Lebron James

The Life, Lessons & Rules for Success

Influential Individuals

Table of Contents

Introduction

To be an expert in your field is admirable. To be the best is rare and remarkable.

LeBron James is a man who is widely considered the world's greatest ever basketball player. He has won gold at the Olympic games; he has led both the Cleveland Cavaliers and the Miami Heat to the NBA Finals and he is the winner of countless accolades in the sport.

But there is so much more to the sporting superstar than what he produces on the basketball court, as considerable as that is. Controversy seems to follow him wherever he goes. This is something that he accepts with equanimity; he is a man who follows his conscience, even if in doing so he ruffles a few feathers.

Further, he is a man who fights for what he believes is right. The word activist conjures all kinds of connotations, some of them negative. But LeBron James does not shy away from activism. Whether it is bringing to notice injustice, particularly against the African American community, highlighting prejudice, or simply making as many lives better as he can, he does his best to uplift and inspire.

Perhaps a part of that desire to give opportunity to others comes from the challenges he faced as a young child. Brought up by a single mother, moving regularly from home to home, he could have fallen off the rails big time. But LeBron got a lucky break. And he took advantage of that to the fullest extent. Now, he seeks to give as many others as he can their own chance to defeat the limitations imposed by their upbringing.

At the age of almost 34, as he begins to consider life after his playing career, the future beckons in many ways. Coach, politician, motivational speaker, pundit, social commentator, activist – and considering LeBron's life so far, possibly a bit of each.

This book looks back on the first 34 years of LeBron's life; the good times and the bad, the successes and the challenges; the adulation and the criticism – criticism, or maybe just envy, that has emerged both from within the basketball world and from wider society, as well.

Read this biography to learn more about the basketball legend, find out how LeBron faced tough times, and consider how his approach to adversity can be adapted to make your own life more fulfilling.

Chapter One: Early Life

"THE REASON WHY I AM WHO I AM TODAY IS BECAUSE I WENT THROUGH THOSE TOUGH TIMES WHEN I WAS YOUNGER."

LeBron Raymone James is Mr. Basketball. From the moment he first rose to national prominence, he has attracted attention and become a role model for a generation of aspiring basketball players. As the top high school basketball player in the entire country during the early part of the millennium, this was a boy who had the world at his feet.

LeBron was born on December 30, 1984 in Akron, Ohio. Akron is not the most noteworthy of cities. The fifth largest in the state, located close to Lake Erie and with a population of just under 750,000 people, it is better known for its manufacturing industries than its sports players. However, today, it is commonly recognized as the birthplace of one of the greatest basketball players in the history of the sport.

His beginnings were not auspicious. His mother, Gloria Marie James, was just 16 years old when she became a single mother. His father, Anthony McClelland, never demonstrated an interest in his young son. Anthony's relationship with Gloria had never been more than casual, and he had acquired a substantial criminal record. He spent many of his son's formative years behind bars.

Those early childhood years were tough for LeBron. The family struggled with money, and a growing boy was a lot to handle for a single mother who was not much more than a girl herself. The two moved from apartment to seedy apartment in the less savory parts of the city, and Gloria struggled to find work, or hold it down when she got a job.

But when LeBron was still young, Gloria realized that she could not offer him the future she wanted for her son. He was already demonstrating sporting prowess, although not yet in the field for which he would become world famous. At this point in time, football was the sport that young LeBron seemed to excel in. It was pretty obvious from a young age that he was going to become a big man, and so it seemed as though he possessed the physical attributes necessary to play this sport at a high level. And so, Gloria accepted an offer from LeBron's football coach, Bruce Kelker, to move in with his family.

When LeBron was nine, he moved in with another coach, Frank Walker – this time without his mother. But the local youth football teacher spotted other talents in young LeBron – talents suited for a sport other than football – and introduced him to a new sport. Basketball.

Lebron quickly took to the sport and soon joined the Northeast Ohio Shooting Stars as part of the Amateur Athletic Union's basketball league. The true stars of the team were four friends – Sian Cotton, Dru Joyce III, Willi McGee, and LeBron James. Led by the self-styled "Fab Four," the team enjoyed local and national success. The boys were inseparable and promised that high school would not see them go their separate ways.

One of the less savory aspects of Akron's history is that it was once home to the USA's largest chapter of the Ku Klux Klan. Those times were past in the mid-to-late nineties when James and his pals were moving on to high school, but even so, when four black friends bitten by the basketball bug chose to go to a largely white, private Catholic high school, the move was seen as a little controversial locally, to say the least.

In his first year at the school, LeBron averaged an astonishing 21 points, plus six rebounds, per game. The school finished the year with a 27–0 win-to-loss record. They came out the comfortable winners of the Division III state title.

During his second year, LeBron's statistics were even better. 25.2 points per game, more than seven rebounds – he once more led his high school to the state championship, this time with a 26–1 record.

Such was the growing reputation of the team that at times the school was forced to play at the University of Akron's Rhodes Arena. The reason? NBA and college scouts, along with numerous alumni, were putting such pressure on ticket sales that the school arena could not cope with demand. Much of that demand was focused on LeBron.

At the end of the season, he became the first sophomore to win two prestigious awards. He was named Ohio Mr. Basketball and was selected for the USA Today All-USA First Team.

By the next season, LeBron was a strapping sixteen-year-old beginning to fill out his lanky frame. Before the year began, Slam Magazine claimed that he could be "the best high school basketball player in America right now." His fame spread further, and later in the season, he became the first high school junior to ever appear on the cover of Sports Illustrated. Although he received much attention, LeBron's feet remained firmly on the ground. (Unless, that is, they were being employed in making a devastating interception or a flamboyant slam dunk.) For the third year in a row, his averages improved. He scored an average of 29 points per game, made 8.3 rebounds, and his assists and steals were increasing.

LeBron was made Ohio Mr. Basketball for the second year in a row and was again selected for the USA Today All-USA First Team. He was also the youngest player to be named as boys' basketball's Gatorade National Player of the Year.

The St. Vincent team that year still performed astonishingly well, with a 23–4 record. However, LeBron began to feel the need for a greater challenge. He petitioned for a change to the eligibility rules of the NBA draft, which at the time required players to be in possession of a minimum of a high school diploma.

For the first time in his sporting career the teen began to feel the pressure. His application to change the rules failed, and he tested the water with marijuana. Constant media attention was beginning to take its toll.

In his senior year, LeBron once more increased his points per game – to 31.6 – his rebounds, and all other aspects of his game. St. Vincent-St. Mary's was also gaining a degree of notoriety. The Fighting Irish began to play further afield, including in some televised games. Such was LeBron's growing fame that Time Warner Cable offered one match on a pay-per-view basis, hoping to cash in on the boy's star appeal.

LeBron's senior year also came with its share of controversy. For his eighteenth birthday, his mother secured a bank loan against his future earnings to buy him a car. Namely, an $80,000 Hummer. The purchase did not go over well with the

Ohio High School Athletic Association, who decided that the Hummer might be counted as a reward for his high school athletic performance. LeBron was cleared of wrongdoing, however, since his mother had been the one to gift him the car.

Then, a local sports store gave him two jerseys whose combined value exceeded the $100 limit that the association allowed as "reward." He had received the jerseys in return for posing for a picture, so it was an easier call for the board to make to say he had broken their rules. He was declared ineligible to play at the high school level any more. And since he still did not have his high school diploma, he could not move yet into the professional sphere.

But in an early sign of LeBron's unwillingness to take crap from anybody, he took the association to court, and won. His suspension was reduced to just two games and he was able to finish the rest of the season.

With unsurprising regularity, he was once more named Ohio Mr. Basketball, made the USA Today team for a third consecutive year (something unprecedented in the history of the organization), and once again won Gatorade National Player of the Year. He was also selected for three end-of-season high school basketball all-star games.

This meant that he lost his National Collegiate Athletic

Association eligibility. However, LeBron had already decided to forego college basketball and head straight for the 2003 NBA draft.

Chapter Two: A History of Activism

"BEING BLACK IN AMERICA IS TOUGH. WE GOT A LONG WAY TO GO FOR US AS A SOCIETY AND FOR US AS AFRICAN AMERICANS UNTIL WE FEEL EQUAL IN AMERICA."

Being recognized as a world superstar in any field brings both responsibilities and opportunities. LeBron regularly uses his status to support causes, although some of them are controversial.

He gained pretty much universal support for his very public criticism of former Los Angeles Clippers' owner, Donald Sterling. He demonstrated a determination to stand up for what he believed was necessary action, even if it could mean the death of his career.

Sterling was always a controversial figure, a man who operated policies in contravention of the spirit, if not the actual wording, of the Fair Housing Act. But it took many years for the wealthy mogul's true side to come out. He was recorded, allegedly, telling his mixed-race girlfriend not to bring any black spectators to the games involving his team. Prior to that, it was more his team's performances that drew attention – to put it bluntly, the Clippers were not very good. The stories that he allegedly made statements to his employees that black and Hispanic families did not make the sort of tenants he wanted were left alone, not pursued against a man of influence and power. Another significant omission to the resume of the property giant was, largely, the fact that he was sued in 2006 by the Justice Department for allegedly operating a policy whereby housing discrimination took place. That is the way of the world for many, who recognize injustice but can do little about it. But LeBron was determined that Sterling was not going to get away with his odious behavior again and said that he would not play in the NBA if Sterling retained his franchise. The authorities listened, and although it was a drawn-out affair, the franchise was eventually sold to a more suitable owner.

Another cause to gain LeBron's significant support began on February 26, 2012, when an unarmed black teenager was shot dead by a neighborhood watch volunteer named George Zimmerman. The boy's crime seemed to amount to wearing a hoodie and carrying some Skittles. Plus, he was sporting a measure of Arizona Iced Tea.

These days, the case of Trayvon Martin is moderately well

known and that is in part due to LeBron James. At the time it occurred, it was one of those cases to be swept under the rug. Zimmerman was eventually charged with the murder of the young boy, but was cleared on the grounds of self-defense. Strange, since recordings of 911 calls indicate that he was chasing the child, who was seeking to get away. But this was Jed Trump's Florida, home of the "Stand Your Ground" law and not a location where the rights of African Americans are especially valued.

Perhaps it is an indication of Zimmerman's outlook that he later tried to auction off the gun that he used to kill Trayvon, calling it an "American Firearm Icon." Nice.

LeBron James took up the cause, using his enormous social media following to publicize the issue. He persuaded his teammates to each don an identical hoodie to the one that Trayvon wore on the night of his murder and then posted a photo of the team to his many millions of fans on social media. He captioned the photo with the slogan: "We Want Justice." Of course, such a move angered right-wing white America, but it achieved his goals of bringing attention to the crime and guiding the subject of African American rights back to the center of public debate.

Other topics on which he has raised concerns and publicized injustices include the War in Darfur, the Michael Brown debacle, and the death of Eric Garner. This last offense saw another black man, this time a 43-year-old, killed by the authorities supposedly there to offer protection.

Garner was killed when arrested after an NYPD officer placed him in a neck lock – something illegal under the laws of constraint by which the force is meant to abide.

The circumstances leading up to Garner's untimely death defy belief. He was arrested for allegedly trying to sell cigarettes unlawfully. Five officers then forced him to ground, with officer Daniel Pantelo delivering the headlock. Garner was heavily outnumbered and claimed at least eleven times that he could not breathe before his head was forced into the ground and he lost consciousness.

Then, he was left untreated for seven minutes while an ambulance arrived, and no attempt was made to give him CPR. Unsurprisingly, he died, and LeBron James' role in making sure that the public was aware of the event contributed to it eventually being properly investigated.

But it is not just the big, front page news causes that the basketball player supports.

He has his own charity, the LeBron James Family Foundation, which supports families in his home town of Akron. The charity holds an annual bike-a-thon to raise money and supports many local causes.

Perhaps most notably, the foundation was a major player in the creation of the "I Promise" Elementary school in Akron. LeBron was, and is, deeply proud of the school, calling its creation the most important professional accomplishment of his life; pretty impressive considering the number of trophies and medals that could line the walls of his home. He takes a particular interest in at-risk children. If one of his "charges" misses school, they receive a voice message urging them to get back as soon as they are well enough. It is a small gesture, but one which might just make the difference between going to school and getting into trouble.

In 2015, he formed a partnership with the University of Akron, which will provide scholarships for up to 2,300 children beginning in 2021.

Then, in 2016, he demonstrated support for another iconic black sportsman and civil rights activist, the legendary Muhammad Ali. The Smithsonian Museum of African History and Culture wished to stage an exhibition in honor of the former world boxing champion and advocate for the rights of African Americans. The $2.5 million LeBron donated ensured that the exhibition would be a success.

The ONEXONE children's charity and Children's Defense Fund also benefit from his patronage.

As we shall see in more detail later, LeBron James is not

without his critics. And those critics were in full force during the release of his 2010 ESPN documentary, *The Decision*, which many saw as self-congratulatory and self-serving. Whether or not that is the case, the millions of dollars made from the show itself and from the advertising revenue were donated by LeBron to charities like After-School All-Stars and the Boys and Girls Clubs of America.

By 2017, his contributions to the community were officially recognized, when he was awarded the J. Walter Kennedy Citizenship Award for his "Outstanding Service and Dedication to the Community." That this award came from the NBA, an organization with whom his relationship was occasionally choppy, was especially gratifying to him.

Chapter Three: Breaking Into The Big Time...And Staying There

"ALL YOUR LIFE YOU ARE TOLD THE THINGS YOU CANNOT DO."

To be honest, making first pick of the NBA draft is a pretty good indicator that a player is a star in the making. But across many walks of life, early promise fails to deliver its full potential. That was something that LeBron James sought hard to avoid.

The boy with the tough upbringing on the harsher streets of Akron was just 19 by the end of his rookie season. Remarkably, he featured in the top five of each major statistical group for rookies. He achieved 5.5 rebounds per game, the fifth best among the newcomers to the league. He found himself in third place overall in assists, averaging 5.9 per game. Then, his scoring record saw him in second place, with 20.9 points per game and he was top among rookie steals, taking possession from the opposition on average 1.65 times per game.

He became only the third player in NBA history to average

more than 20 points, five assists, and five rebounds per game in his rookie season, placing himself among NBA greats Oscar Robertson and Michael Jordan.

He even became the youngest player in NBA history to score more than 40 points in a single game when he scored 41 in a game against New Jersey.

But something that made LeBron's first season even more remarkable was that he achieved the above while playing for a distinctly average team. In fact, worse than average. Take him out of their line up and the Cavaliers had little else to offer. The season before LeBron joined them, they had won just 17 games.

With LeBron's help, that figure was more than doubled in the 2003/2004 season, and the team ended up with a respectable, but far from dominant, 35–47 record.

Given all of that, it was of little surprise that he was awarded the Eddie Gottlieb Trophy when named the 2003/4 got milk? Rookie of the Year. It was not a difficult or surprising choice. It was not a close call. It wasn't really even a competition. Although Carmelo Anthony, of Denver, scored 430 points in the race, Dwayne Wade was such a distant third that he finished with 117.

LeBron James scored 508 points in the vote, which reflects the views of sportswriters and broadcasters in the US and

Canada. 118 votes are cast for the position of first place. LeBron secured an astonishing 78 of these. Considering that local pressures and interests push and pull the basketball-supporting public, as well as the professionals surrounding the game, such a score is quite remarkable.

Although this breakthrough season was already remarkable, the media touted LeBron's performance as nearly god-like. There can be, within press circles, a tendency to build people up to a far greater extent than is justified. Then, when they fail to make the impossible grade that has been targeted for them, recording that failure makes a better story. The higher you rise, the further you fall. With this in mind, LeBron was being touted as the "chosen one" in media circles. Any failure on his part would be the story of the year.

LeBron's fall from grace could have happened while he played for the national team between 2004 and 2006. Firstly, at the 2004 Athens Olympics, he was part of the team defeated 91–89 by Argentina in the semifinals. It was a thrilling match, and a huge shock. This defeat meant that the US basketball team could only secure a bronze medal.

While this would be a noteworthy achievement for almost any other sports player in any other field, for the US basketball team, it represented a huge disappointment. It was only the third time in Olympic history that the US hadn't won gold in basketball – and the first time ever since the team had been composed of NBA players.

That disappointment was replicated at the World Championship two years later, when once more, defeat in the semifinals, this time to a very strong Greek team, pushed LeBron and his teammates to a new low.

But it is a sign of the mental strength of LeBron James that he took such disappointment, and such media criticism, in his stride. The US team would go on to win the next two Olympic golds – with LeBron's help.

The international stage was not the only one on which LeBron could have failed, however. Second NBA seasons are notoriously challenging. Opponents know all about you, expectations can rise impossibly high. But LeBron was up to meeting every challenge the basketball world could throw at him.

Soon, he was being talked about everywhere and everyone seemed to recognize his prowess. George Karl, coach of the Denver Nuggets, admitted that LeBron was a great player – not a great player for his age and inexperience, but a truly great player – saying, "He's the exception to almost every rule."

He was soaring to ever-greater heights, scoring a record-breaking 56 points in one match against the Toronto Raptors.

His averages, all of which improved on those he achieved in his rookie season, saw him selected to his first All-NBA team. The Cavaliers, largely thanks to LeBron, enjoyed a winning season, 42–40, although they did fail to make the playoffs.

A further accolade followed in 2006, when LeBron was named the NBA All-Star Game Most Valuable Player for the season. He had led the Cavaliers to their first playoffs in almost a decade, and although they fell to the Detroit Pistons in the second round, LeBron's performance was impressive.

The following season, Lebron struggled and his average declined, with some commentators blaming a lack of focus and effort. But the Cavaliers still qualified for the playoffs, and this time, success was forthcoming. In the final match of the Eastern Conference championship, revenge against the Pistons was secured. In a performance that was called "one of the greatest moments of postseason history," LeBron scored a remarkable 48 points, with nine rebounds and seven assists. He achieved the astonishing feat of scoring 29 out of 30 of his team's final points.

In the 2007/2008 season, LeBron eased past Brad Dougherty to become the Cavaliers' all-time leading scorer, a feat which he achieved in over a hundred fewer games than the legend he surpassed. This proved that he was not just a player with fancy moves but no real substance. LeBron was an exceptional player with the stats to prove it.

2008/2009 marked a high for both LeBron and his team. They reached the Conference Finals led by their own shooting star, who was described as "having what is arguably the greatest individual season in history," by no lesser a name than John Hollinger. That this comment was followed up with the phrase "and its time we gave him his due for it" indicates the blatant dislike and disparagement of LeBron that was often displayed by the media.

However, the basketball star had more important things on his mind than snarky reporters.

On July 1, 2010, LeBron James became a free agent. Undoubtedly, the phone rang constantly with offers from other franchises. Who would not want such a superstar among their ranks?

July 1, 2010 was the day that marked the beginning of the next stage in Lebron James' remarkable career.

Chapter Four: Out Of Favor – The Heat Is On In Miami

"I LIKE CRITICISM. IT MAKES YOU STRONG."

Do the ends justify the means? A tough question, but if those ends include $6 million dollars for good causes, and the means is simply a way of telling a story that will be told anyway, then few could argue against the notion that the ends do indeed justify the means.

People change their jobs all the time. Moving from General Motors to Chrysler as CEO would be seen as either a good career move, or a bad one. But it would not cause the burning of cars, accusations of betrayal and the sort of venom that LeBron faced when he decided to move to the Miami Heat to play alongside superstar Dwayne Wade.

Perhaps the manner of the announcement played a part in the misplaced hysteria. The ESPN special, *The Decision*, a program referred to as a "self-worshipping made-for-TV special" by Greg Cote of the Miami Herald, on which James made his announcement did seem a little self-aggrandizing, but it also raised the aforementioned $6 million, which was donated to charity.

Back home, the Cavaliers prepared to move on. They had assumed that LeBron would continue to star for them with a new contract. By this point, he had been awarded the MVP accolade twice, and at the age of 25, was a player in his prime, an Olympic gold medal winner, a man who turned matches. But they knew his loss was a possibility and decided not to dwell on the unwanted turn of events.

Still, to many of their fans, LeBron had turned traitor. He had taken money over loyalty, the prospect of straightforward championships over hard work and perseverance with a strong, but not strongest, team. But then, that is something sports stars do across the world. If you are the best, you want to be playing alongside the best. You want to win titles. And as many awards as had made their way into LeBron's hands, what he really wanted was an NBA championship. It seemed like that was something he might not achieve if he remained in Cleveland.

Down in Miami, reactions were mixed. Overnight, the Heat became the strongest team on the planet. Some of their fans rejoiced. Others were less sure. Would the egos of Wade and James ever become compatible? Was LeBron as arrogant as many claimed – Greg Cote thought so, dubbing the superstar "the man who calls himself king," and if so, was he the kind of player Miami wanted? A great team is more than the sum of its parts – and especially more than a single player. Teamwork, understanding, esprit de corps – all of these contributed to success. Having the best players helped, but it was not a guarantee of glory.

Even those who had no direct interest in either Cleveland or Miami wanted their say. Andrew Wojnarowski with Yahoo! Sports opined, "The Championship of Me became the Championship of Flee. Divorce your childhood sweetheart on National Television." He continued, "…this felt like a cloistered teenager picking a party school for college."

For James, the move was about achieving something he felt was just beyond Cleveland at that time. The NBA Championship. Along with Chris Bosh, Miami now boasted the first, fourth, and fifth picks from the 2003 draft. Three superstars in their prime.

"You become a superstar individually, but you become a champion as a team," said LeBron with a hint of arrogance. Or was it just confidence? There exists a fine line between the two. He stated that the decision to move was driven by the desire to become a champion. The three superstars simply wished to play together. They were not doing if for the money. In fact, they could earn more by staying with their respective teams.

Still, despite this explanation, criticism was rampant. During *The Decision*, LeBron uttered the that he was "taking his talents to South Beach." The phrase became a byword for derision. It entered common parlance, coming to represent a lack of loyalty, a lack of love for home.

Later, he accepted that maybe he could have made his announcement differently, but the criticism that poured down on him was completely out of scale with the scope of his "crime." A free agent, he had not reneged on a contract. He had not murdered anyone, he had not stolen property. He had not defrauded the IRS. No, he had taken his considerable talent to a new setting, to provide a new challenge in an environment where success was likely to be more forthcoming.

He also suggested that the extent of the criticism may have had racial overtones, which could well bear some truth, as unpalatable as the accusation might be. As one might imagine, this suggestion only earned his greater criticism. Where racism does exist, bringing attention to it can be a truly incendiary action. But as we've learned, LeBron James is not one to shy away from the truth just to keep everyone comfortable.

LeBron played with the Miami Heat for four seasons. His first season was one of extreme criticism and scrutiny. The team struggled to find their footing and LeBron himself seemed to be heavily affected by the negativity thrown his way, playing aggressively and angrily. The Heat managed to clinch a winning season after their shaky start, largely thanks to LeBron, but they were eventually defeated in the Finals. Critics, to no one's surprise, blamed this loss on LeBron, whose performance was less than stellar.

However, back-to-back championships followed this first season of defeat. LeBron managed to shake off the negativity and find his stride once again, racking up numerous awards and leading the Heat to victory not once, but twice.

As critics were keen to point out, this success was a result of the team, not of any one player's performance. But there can be little doubt that having three of the finest players on the planet played its own significant part in the Miami Heat's success. Whether or not there were tensions off court, when they were on it, team spirit was strong, with the superstars, especially LeBron, contributing heavily to the team's overall success.

Still, the Heat were treated to an overwhelmingly amount of negativity. Booed at every quarter, seen as the pariahs of the sport in every city outside of Miami, whether the success was ultimately worth the pain is something only the players can decide upon. At the end of the day, they would probably conclude that it was.

During his final season with Miami Heat, a highlight for LeBron was a record-breaking 61 personal points haul in a game against the Charlotte Bobcats. But the season was, after the highs of the previous two, disappointing. Injuries had decimated the squad, and although they reached the playoffs, the team was eliminated in the Finals by the San Antonio Spurs.

James decided that he had come to the end of his time with Miami and opted out of his contract. His announcement that he planned to return to play for the Cleveland Cavaliers was more quietly made than his decision to leave had been four years previously. It was also much better received. It appeared as though four seasons of criticism and hassle were coming to an end.

After all, everyone loves the prodigal son. Everyone loves a boy who comes home.

Chapter Five: Coming Home

"I DON'T NEED TOO MUCH. GLAMOR AND ALL THAT STUFF DON'T EXCITE ME.
I'M JUST GLAD I HAVE THE GAME OF BASKETBALL IN MY LIFE."

LeBron anticipated his first game back with the Cleveland
Cavaliers with some excitement. "I am coming back to
Cleveland not just a different player, but a rejuvenated
person," he said.

That first game was against the New York Knicks, and LeBron
recognized that he was now more than just a member of the
team, more than even simply its star player. With two
championships squeezed under his belt, fitting in around the
many other accolades he had gained, he knew that he would
be expected to deliver both on the court and off it. "I do have a
role to mentor now," he said. "That is something I will be
taking seriously."

With LeBron in their ranks, the Cavaliers had systematically
moved up the rankings from also-rans, to playoff contenders,
to Eastern champions. The only thing that they had failed to
achieve was the NBA title itself.

Once LeBron left, his team had failed to even make the playoffs for four consecutive seasons. There was a lot of work to be done. During the first season back, there was a definite improvement in the Cavaliers, thanks in no small part to LeBron's influence, and the team for whom failure to match potential was starting to become an unwanted label, showed up at last.

To be fair, it was not a one-man team – nothing like. Along with the re-signing of LeBron James, the Cavaliers brought in Kevin Love. These two joined guard Kyrie Irving to make a "big three" of All-Star players.

More than that, it was a season dogged by injury, so a 53–29 regular season return was a great feat. It was also enough to propel them to the top of the Central Division. There were some, the usual critics, who had tried to label LeBron as a spent force when he moved on from the Miami Heat; there was no better way to demonstrate that there was life in the old legs still.

In fact, the Cavaliers continued with their good form, making it all the way to the Championship finals, where their opponents were the Golden State Warriors. The Cavaliers were eventually defeated 4-2, which marked the beginning of a period of rivalry between these two teams for dominance of the NBA.

During the next season, the Cavaliers entered the tenth game with a comfortable 8–1 record. But that game and the next (a narrow defeat against the Detroit Pistons) told LeBron that there was still much work to be done.

He felt that it was down to character, not skill. "We are too relaxed and too nice," he said at a post-match press conference. "It is a mental toughness, going out and doing your job. Doing it at a high level and preparing that way before the tip even happens."

He was not afraid to say it as he saw it. He might be older, and he might have the confidence of championships behind him, but he was not afraid to cause controversy. Especially if he believed it was for the good of the team. "We have got some guys who will do it, and some guys who do not do it consistently enough," he continued.

One of the strengths of LeBron James, throughout his career and indeed his life before that, is a willingness to step up to the plate and take responsibility. Setting the highest possible standards for himself enabled him to take the often unfair criticism that came his way. It also allowed him to aim for the highest goal at every stage of his life.

"So definitely myself and the rest of the bigs, we have got to challenge ourselves. It has got to come from within sometimes," he asserted.

LeBron's words hit home. From that point onwards, the team began to find consistency. Close to unbeatable at home, the team was also a force to be reckoned with on the road. November saw them unbeaten after LeBron's speech to the press, with an overall 11– 3 record. December saw a small slip, but they were back to their best by January, with a 7–1 record on the road. The team was on a roll, and it seemed certain that they would once more win the Eastern Division Championship.

Although pressure began to mount as the season reached its climax, they were already home and dry, and the playoffs awaited.

They reached the final, where once more, the Golden State Warriors awaited. It seemed as though history was about to repeat itself. 3–1 down after four games, it seemed certain that Cleveland would once more fail to raise their game when they needed it most. They had not secured the NBA title in 52 years, after all.

By Game Seven, though, it was back to 3–3. It was down to this. The Championship would be decided by one game.

A superstar does not choose to be a such. If they did, there would be many more of them about. Circumstances and skill combine to deliver such status. In a team sport, a superstar makes a difference but does not win championships alone.

Much of the criticism delivered to LeBron was that he had turned the Cavaliers into a one-man team, that his personality had squashed others to the side.

Game Seven proved that that criticism was not true. In fact, it knocked back nearly every accusation critics had hurled at LeBron.

The victory that came from that game was a team effort, one sprinkled with the fairy dust of superstardom. LeBron James played all but two minutes of that game, a physical and mental achievement, under the pressure of the biggest game in the Cavaliers' long history, of astonishing proportions. Kevin Love had been beset by injury for most of the season. His time with the Cavaliers had failed to deliver its promise. Finally, in that seventh game, he hit top form. The other member of the "big three," Kyrie Irving had also been sidelined for the best part of the season through injury. Irving still suffered from his injured knee but came through in that game with his best performance that season.

Every other member of team played their part on that court. But the cook manipulating that recipe of greatness, applying and measuring and stirring, was LeBron James. He was top scorer, took most rebounds, made most passes, and blocked most shots for the entire series. In the final game, he scored 27 points, made 11 rebounds, and provided 11 assists. Leading by personality. Leading by example.

"My guys believe in me as their leader," he said after the game. "They allow me to lead. I was just true to that. I knew what I was capable of doing and my guys allowed me to lead them for 48 minutes. I gave everything that I had for 48 minutes."

Let us consider for a moment the reaction when, six years previously, LeBron had signed, a free agent, with the Miami Heat. Traitor, money grabber, arrogant delusionist. The insults flew like the baskets he scored.

But this was a man who, entering that final game of the season, had already achieved everything possible in the sport. Two NBA championships, two gold Olympic medals, more money than he could ever spend, global fame, and, among those who matter most, adoration. More personal accolades, trophies, and awards than could be adequately described here.

Why would one more win matter so much? How could it? Because he cared. Because, above all else, LeBron James loved Cleveland, felt an attachment to it that went way beyond bouncing a basketball. He knew how much sealing a championship meant to the people of Cleveland. How it would, for a while at least, offer hope, a relief from the tedium and poverty of everyday life.

"Our fans...it was for them!" he roared as tears filled his eyes. For all the criticism he'd received, for all the anger they'd shown him when he left for Miami, LeBron James wanted nothing more than to bring joy to the Cavaliers' fans. His own joy at being able to achieve this feat was palpable as he fell to the floor of the arena in celebration.

It was his greatest moment. The greatest moment of perhaps the greatest player the sport has ever known.

Unfortunately, in the 2018 NBA Finals, Cleveland, reigning champions, were swept away in a 4–0 defeat by the Golden State Warriors. It was a humiliating experience.

In an interview after the devastating loss for the Cavaliers, their star man revealed a reason behind his own disappointing form (although, his performance was still astounding).

He had been playing three matches with a broken hand. Remember, this is a man who does not need money. He holds championship medals galore, along with his two Olympic golds. He did not drop out and let his teammates face the Warriors without him, although it would be easy for him to have done so. He did not leap at the first opportunity to make excuses. He simply, calmly put into perspective his own contribution to his team's disappointment. Hardly the behavior of a self-publicizing body of arrogance.

But nothing is ever that straightforward when it comes to

LeBron. Many reports offer the same reason for that break in his hand. Apparently, it occurred when he punched a whiteboard in the locker room following defeat in Game One of the series against the Warriors. So, the impetuous action of a spoiled man child? Or just a sign of passion and commitment, anger at missed opportunity?

Interestingly, LeBron seems to recognize that he sometimes acts without thinking, the passion and instinct that made him the great of the sport sometimes letting him down in his everyday life. In that interview at the end of the series, he was sheepish, but not repentant about his damaged hand, simply saying, "I let the emotions get the best of me and pretty much played the last three games with a broken hand."

Many fans fear that LeBron may have played his last game for the Cleveland Cavaliers. Others suspect he may have played his last game in the NBA full stop. That other challenges now tempt him away. We will consider this more in the final chapter, but even if his Cavaliers' career is over, for the second time, even if it did end in pain and defeat, yet again, LeBron arrived at a team who was underperforming and turned it around. Just like he did as a near rookie with the national team, as he did the first time with Cleveland, and as he did with the star-strewn might of the Miami Heat.

Chapter Six: The Time That Mattered Most

"I HEAR MY FRIENDS AND MY MOM TELL ME I'M SPECIAL, BUT HONESTLY, I STILL DON'T GET IT."

With the perspective of an adult, LeBron James is able to look back at his formative years. As we have seen throughout this biography, he is a man deeply committed to his community, to young people, and the rights of the African American community. Just as he is committed to them, so they are supporters of his. In fact, the word "supporter" understates the importance of LeBron James in many young people's lives. In an area where basketball is like a religion, a religion with new followers joining every day – especially after the success of recent years – then James is more than just a sportsman. He is a role model, a person to look up to, an icon. That carries responsibility. James is variously criticized for removing himself from his roots, for enjoying the spoils of his success. That criticism is deeply unfair and unjustified, because he is a man, increasingly as he gets older, who plays a hugely influential role for good in his home environment.

One of the tasks he gives himself is to use his fame and his reputation for good, by giving, a few times every year, motivational talks to young people.

Imagine being a fourteen-year-old on the cusp of adolescence, facing the decision of whether to commit to school or take the easy way out. And there, talking to you and your friends, is a giant – both physically and metaphorically. A man who, like you, grew up in difficult circumstances, who has not always made the best decisions, but who through hard work, intelligence, and commitment has made it very much to the top.

You would listen.

It's interesting that when LeBron gives these talks, he doesn't spend time talking about 2003, when he made number one pick of the senior draft, when he met his wife-to-be, and when his life really took off. He doesn't talk about winning titles and making championships. No, he talks about the fourth grade.

A bit of context is needed here. Gloria James, LeBron's mother, was, as you will recall 16 when LeBron was born. In those days, they lived in a big, old house down a dirt road in Akron. Gloria returned to school and LeBron was looked after by Gloria's mother, Freda, and grandmother.

Gloria's grandmother died soon after LeBron was born. He

never really got the opportunity to know her. But they could manage. Just about. Then, when LeBron was just three, Freda died suddenly, succumbing to a heart attack on Christmas day.

Within the space of a couple of years the heart was ripped out of the family. Security, income, experience – they were all gone. Gloria, along with her two brothers, tried to keep together, but they lacked the skills and the money. Heating alone cost a fortune.

It was as a result of those sudden deaths, and the consequences they caused, that Gloria and LeBron moved from house to house, sleeping at friends' places when they could get nothing more permanent. It was everything a young child did not need. The benefits of an extended family were gone. There was no home, no roots, no stability, and nowhere the young boy could call his own. Gloria did her absolute best, but she was still a girl herself, one with plenty of growing up of her own left to do. Several years passed this same way. And so, we reach fourth grade. The eight-year-old was already nearly as tall as his mother. And when local football coach Bruce Kelker was searching for a running back, Bron Bron (as his mother called him) demonstrated very quickly that he had the pace and balance to play there.

Kelker had a novel way of selecting his young team. He

would visit areas of Akron, and take a look at the kids playing. If he thought he spotted some potential, athleticism, speed, or size, he would call the kids together and set them off on a race. The winner would, he said, become a part of his team. The race he organized the day he saw LeBron for the first time was easily decided, the tall boy winning by a mile. But kids' sport in America is competitive (mainly for the adults involved) , and Akron was no different in that respect. Coaches can sometimes forget that they are dealing with youngsters, and (dare it be said) take matters a little too seriously.

Soon, the coaches of beaten teams started to complain about LeBron's size. They claimed he was overage, or that it was just unfair that such a physical oddity should be permitted to destroy their teams. Imagine hearing that as a self-conscious eight-year-old. A boy who, for any outward cockiness, lacked self-esteem. LeBron, just like any other kid, wanted to be normal, and so responded to these comments by sloping his shoulders and huddling his knees.

"What the hell are you doing?" the coach asked. When LeBron stated that he was trying to blend in, to avoid being noticed, his mentor said something that would stay with him throughout his life: "You ain't never going to blend in. And that can be a good thing."

As you might recall, LeBron and his mother moved in with Bruce Kelker for a time. It might seem an odd arrangement, but for a while, it worked. Kelker lived with his girlfriend in one half of the home, while Gloria and LeBron took a room in the other. But soon, having two families under one roof proved too much, and it was Frank Walker's turn to house the boy. However, Walker already had a family, and space was tight in his home. He had no spare room, nowhere that could house two additional people. This time, his mother stayed with a friend, and young LeBron shared with Walker's son, Frankie Jr.

When he relates this tale, James tells his audience that this was a crucial turning point in his life. Stability returned. The Walkers made sure that James did his homework, undertook his chores, went to school. They enlisted him in a ground-breaking institution which took a holistic approach to learning, a method that suited him better than listening to a teacher drone on all day.

As he is finishing the story, LeBron James, probably the greatest basketball player there has ever been, says something that he hopes will prove the importance of schooling to those who are listening, but teetering on the edge of spoiling their life chances.

He tells of two trips with his school. In the first, he is

disruptive and troublesome. A year later, the teachers are so worried about what he might get up to that they consider refusing to take him.

But that was year when he had embraced basketball, taken responsibility (as assistant coach to an Under 8 team), and learned to be a part of a family. The teachers need not have worried.

There is always an opportunity to turn your life around, the message states. You just have to make the effort.

Just as he is making the effort, willingly and in his own time, in an attempt to help those who might end up on the path he so nearly followed. LeBron is, of course, too worldly to believe that every face in front of him, lapping up his words, will leave his talk a reformed character. But he knows that some will, and that is enough.

Chapter Seven: Rules for Success

Rule One: Learn From Others

No-one is born with all the answers, which is why having mentors or guides are valuable to achieve success. LeBron went to Miami Heat and was guided by Pat Riley and Dwayne Wade. It was through their advice and experience, LeBron learned how to play at a champion's level and how to win. When he left and went back to Cleveland, he took all his new knowledge and experience back with him.

Learning from others is vital for success as it teaches you new insights and ideas that you may not have been exposed to. It keeps you open-minded and accepting of other opinions and perspectives. The experience of others allows you to move forward more efficiently as you learn from their mistakes and helps you avoid the pitfalls you may have fallen into otherwise. Everyone has a story to tell and by talking with different people, you can learn about new experiences and points of views. This will help with both your personal and professional development.

Rule Two: Earn Respect

Since he was 17-years-old, LeBron James had to constantly prove he was worthy of all the hype that surrounded him. To earn respect, he had to put himself in challenging situations and push himself forward every day to become successful. He had plenty of critics and pressure throughout his career, yet it never prevented him from working hard and pouring effort and time into his profession. The strong work ethics that he applied both at the beginning of his career and today helped elevate him to be considered as the face of the NBA. LeBron's relentlessly proactive approach made him one of the world's most successful and well-respected basketball players. Respect isn't given lightly and it takes dedication and commitment to a cause to get it. You also need self-respect and belief in your abilities before you can expect others to respect you back. Respect yourself and others around you will follow suit.

Rule Three: Support Others Around You

Personal success is wonderful and satisfying. However, most of our individual successes are a product of the people around us. When you help other people around you to achieve their goals, especially when you work in a team, this can have a huge impact and help you achieve more in the long run. A game of basketball can never be won with just one person alone and depends on the greatness of everyone in the team. The same applies anywhere in life and by supporting your team, you can set your goals bigger and higher.

LeBron demands excellence in himself, but also encourages it from the people around him. Thanks to his influence, many of his past and current teammates have had the best moments of their career while playing with LeBron. As he once said, "I think, team first. It allows me to succeed, and it allows my team to succeed."

Rule Four: Embrace Challenges

No matter how tough things get, LeBron takes it in his stride. Before he became a professional basketball player, he grew up without a father, skipped school, and had days of uncertainty about where he and his mum would live next. Later in his career, while playing for the Cleveland Cavaliers, LeBron bought them back from a 3-1 deficit in the finals against the Golden State Warriors. That year, the Golden State Warriors had won a record 73 times. It was no easy feat yet LeBron and his teammates remained positive and worked together to achieve what seemed almost impossible.

Challenges are a part of the road to success and the difference between those who succeed and those who don't is their willingness to take them on. It won't always go your way, yet staying cool and positive will help you do your best every time and learn the valuable lessons failure brings.

Rule Five: Let Go of Grudges

Holding onto grudges hurts no-one other than yourself and

prevents you from moving forward to better things. When LeBron left the Cleveland Cavaliers to play for Miami Heat, the Cavaliers' owner, Dan Gilbert, wrote an aggressive and harsh letter about LeBron. However, after some time at Miami Heat, LeBron returned to play at the Cavaliers. Rather than allowing the grudge to come in between them, LeBron met with Gilbert to talk about their differences and push aside any past bitterness.

Personality clashes are a fact of life and rarely can we push ourselves outside our comfort zone without meeting some sort of conflict. By understanding that this is normal, it can help to not allow these conflicts to get the best of you and instead, accept them as part of moving forward and upward. If you can move past grudges, the better your chances of success.

Rule Six: Tell Your Story

One of the reasons LeBron is so successful is not just because he is an incredible, world-class player. He also exudes personality, which makes him instantly relatable and interesting to watch. LeBron released a documentary on his upbringing in Cleveland, called 'More Than a Game'. It included stories from his childhood and interviews with people who know him, which revealed an intimate and personal side of LeBron. After the documentary launched, LeBron was considered a positive role model and an inspiration.

By telling people your story - truly being yourself - they can see your authentic side and connect with you better. Being honest about who you are, helps you build genuine relationships with people you meet. If you can accept your own past and acknowledge that you are the product of it, then it means you take a huge step towards happiness and ultimately being successful. You can only be truly happy by being yourself and not trying to be someone you're not.

Rule Seven: Work Hard Consistently

In order to have success, you must be prepared to work hard and work hard consistently. Having a few days of solid productivity followed by a period of relaxation won't push you to the high standards required for success. LeBron embraces this lesson and is known for his consistently high-level performances. From the beginning of his career to all the following seasons, whether playing for the Cavaliers or Miami Heat, LeBron has constantly raised the bar and set higher standards both for himself and other players. Throughout his career, LeBron has won three NBA championships, four Most Valuable Player awards, two Olympic gold medals, among other awards.

Even if you are successful now, it's not a reason to stop pushing yourself and seeing how far you can go. LeBron showcases the importance of continuously doing your best and pushing your limits if you want to achieve your goals and be successful.

Rule Eight: Do What is Right for You

When LeBron made the decision to leave the Cleveland Cavaliers and move to Miami Heat, he was met with backlash and a storm of negative media coverage. However, rather than get caught up in all the outrage and doing what others thought was best, he focused on doing what he felt was right for him. In the end, it turned out to be a good career move. He learned a lot while playing for Heat and eventually returned to Cavaliers with refined skills and more knowledge than ever before. It allowed him to grow professionally and become even more successful.

People may try and change your mind about your decisions or think they know what is best for you, but if you feel that you are doing what is right, then stick to your guns. It's your life and your success, so it's vital you do what's best for you in order to achieve your goals.

Rule Nine: Accept Failure

Even great sportsmen like LeBron experience failure from time to time. The main thing is how they view it and learn from it. LeBron's success rate in the NBA finals is 33%, which means he fails in two-thirds of his games. However, perfection is never the goal and LeBron proves that by being the best player in the world.

During the 2011 NBA finals between Miami Heat and the Dallas Mavericks, Heat lost 4-2. It was a devastating blow for LeBron who was criticized for playing passively and ineffectively. From that one game, his reputation was cracked and his performance became the butt of several jokes. While it was an unpleasant experience for LeBron, he gave himself some time to withdraw and reflect upon what happened. Afterward, he accepted he hadn't played to his usual standards and decided that he had to improve his performance next time.

Rule Ten: Learn from the Past

Learn from the past - but don't dwell on it. Your experiences can be a valuable teacher and time reflecting on how you would do things differently can be helpful to learn how to approach similar situations better the next time. However, don't obsess over how things could have been - the "if only" line of thinking is more harmful than it is good. Instead, focus on the positives and the lessons you learned. Making mistakes is fundamental in achieving success.

LeBron learned several lessons from his past experiences and while he acknowledges he would do things differently if he could do it again, he also draws lessons from the decisions he's made. He once said about his time at Miami Heat, "these past four years helped raise me into who I am. I became a better player and man. Without the experiences I had there, I wouldn't be able to do what I'm doing today."

Chapter Eight: What The Future Holds

"THERE'S THAT MOMENT EVERY MORNING WHEN YOU LOOK IN THE MIRROR: ARE YOU COMMITTED, OR ARE YOU NOT?"

LeBron James enjoys a positive personal life. He married his long-term girlfriend, Savannah, on September 14, 2013. They have three children; two sons – LeBron Jr. and Bryce Maximus – and a daughter, Zhuri, the latest addition to the family. LeBron is a great benefactor, seeking to give back to the community in which he was raised. He is also a very wealthy man in his own right. He made the Forbes' Richest Young Celebrities list by the age of 20. By the next year, 2006, he was topping it. His contract when he joined the Miami Heat in 2010 was estimated at around $120 million, and on his return to the Cavaliers, he picked up a $100 million three-year deal. Both of those franchises will, of course, consider that money well spent.

Like most leading sportsmen today, his salary represents only a small percentage of his total income. He endorses many global products, earning millions in the process. Beats by Dre, Coca-Cola, Intel, Verizon, and Kia Motors all boost his bursting bank balance. He also has a deal with Nike, a lifetime contract which could ultimately earn the superstar a cool $1 billion.

The player's total worth is impossible to know for sure. Forbes, as reliable a source as any, estimated that his earnings in 2017 were around $87 million. These are added to a net worth now estimated to be something in the region of $400 million. A figure that looks certain to increase. Not bad for a boy from the back streets of Akron.

As Lebron James contemplates the latter stages of his playing career, the fact that his interests stretch far and wide for him will provide the motivation to take his life to its next stage. We have seen his determination to stand up for the rights of the victims, the repressed, the downtrodden. A career in politics is not out of the question. He would certainly make an imposing figure delivering a speech.

His habit of telling it as it is might not be normal behavior for a politician, but it would certainly go over well with many of the public, if not his spin-ridden political opponents. Whether, though, he could live with the hypocrisy of high office is a tougher challenge to face.

If LeBron selects such a direction for his next career path, he starts with an early advantage. He has already earned a place in Time Magazine's "The 1oo Most Influential People" chart in 2017, gaining a glowing homage written by Rita Dove, a poet laureate and Pulitzer Prize-winning author.

And prior to that, in 2016, he saw what many have come to fear in the presidency of Donald Trump.

At this point on time, the election had not been secured, but LeBron's appearance on the cover of yet another illustrious magazine, this time Sports Illustrated, saw him wearing a safety pin. In 2016, a safety pin became an unspoken message of support and allegiance to those who were likely to suffer should Trump end up in the White House. His fears, many would argue, have come to fruition.

The threat minorities, women, immigrants, and others on the margins faced has been realized. It will be a small, but nevertheless important, comfort to such people to know that they have the backing of some influential people, among them LeBron James.

If that is a route he ultimately chooses, in all likelihood, his commitment and passion will see him gain the same degrees of success he achieved on the indoor courts of the NBA.

But it is not just that passion and that commitment that underpinned his success in sport and is likely to do the same in whatever he chooses next. His colleagues and opponents all speak of his astonishing intelligence. In fact, two kinds of intelligence.

He possesses the instinctive ability to read games, to process information at great speed and make the right decisions. Perhaps it is this that leads him to occasionally speak out apparently without giving himself time for reflection. But that intelligence is not without precedent among sporting superstars.

To be the best takes more than just talent. More than just commitment. More even than passion, although all three of those elements are present in the strongest performers in any discipline. The very best are clever people. It is an often-reported fact that LeBron James can recall every play in the manual without reference to paper files or laptop screens. That ability to learn and understand will serve him well in whatever the future holds.

Imagine him as an administrator in basketball, or sport in general. We could see him sweeping bureaucratic obstinacy aside, refusing to tolerate the corruption that infiltrates some sports, such as soccer.

Or as a coach. The best players do not always make the best coaches. Sometimes they cannot get down to the level of mere mortals in their teams. For LeBron James, that is not likely to be the case. He has demonstrated, especially in the latter part of his career, a considerable ability to motivate others.

With his instinct and almost photographic recall supporting this, we could see him working to precise detail on the practice court, and be flexible and adaptive in the match situation, anticipating problems and instilling changes to address these.

Staying with the sport, as a broadcaster, he would be intelligent and interesting to listen to, with a ready supply of facts to liven up commentary.

But another strong possibility exists as a future career for LeBron James. One in which he has already dabbled.

The star is considering a career in entertainment, following the likes of The Rock and, perhaps less auspiciously, OJ Simpson. Not only does he act, but he also operates as a producer. Among his works to date are the 2014 film *Survivor's Remorse*, the 2015 film *Trainwreck*, and an appearance in the second film of the *Space Jam* franchise.

The glamor of the silver screen would sit well on him. He is a natural in front of the camera, exuding self-confidence and humor. The passion he portrays on the court is well served by the camera, and as a global superstar, he has the sort of pulling power to enable him to attract the biggest stars in the world.

And of course, LeBron is already a highly successful business man in his own right. Who is to say that he will not expand in this aspect of his life? He runs a production company, Springhill Entertainment, which he co-owns with Maverick Carter, his business partner. He also holds a significant share in LRMR Management. This is a sports marketing company which is part-owned by James and Carter along with Randy Mims and Rich Paul.

It may be that we are getting ahead of ourselves. LeBron James is only in his early thirties. He is fit, strong, and intelligent. His passion appears no less diminished that it was when, as a nine-year-old, he was introduced to the sport. He could still have two, three, even five years left at the top, whether with the Cavaliers or elsewhere.

Whatever route LeBron James chooses; he is certain to have the best chance of making it a success. Just as he has done on the basketball court. That iconic Number 23 jersey will be forever ingrained in the annals of sporting history.

Thanks for checking out my book. I hope you found this of value and enjoyed it. If this was the case, head to my author page for more like this. Before you go, I have one small favor to ask…

Would you take 60 seconds and write a quick review about this book?

Reviews are the best way for independent authors (like me) to get noticed, sell more books, and it gives me the motivation to continue producing. I also read every review and use the feedback to write future revisions – and even future books. Thanks again.

Chapter Nine: Playing Career Awards And Highlights

- Three-time NBA All-Star Game MVP (2006, 2008, 2018)

- Twelve-time All-NBA First Team (2006, 2008–2018)

- Fourteen-time NBA All-Star (2005–2018)

- J. Walter Kennedy Citizenship Award (2017)

- Two-time AP Athlete of the Year (2013, 2016)

- Three-time NBA champion (2012, 2013, 2016) (twice with the Miami Heat, once with the Cleveland Cavaliers)

- Three-time NBA Finals MVP (2012, 2013, 2016)

- Two-time Sports Illustrated Sportsperson of the Year (2012, 2016)

- NBA All-Defensive Second Team (2014)

- Five-time NBA All-Defensive First Team (2009–2013)

- Four-time NBA Most Valuable Player (2009, 2010, 2012, 2013)

- USA Basketball Male Athlete of the Year (2012)

- NBA scoring champion (2008)

- Two-time All-NBA Second Team (2005, 2007)

- NBA Rookie of the Year (2004)

- Naismith Prep Player of the Year (2003)

- McDonald's All-American Game MVP (2003)

- Two-time Mr. Basketball USA (2002, 2003)

- Three-time Ohio Mr. Basketball (2001, 2002, 2003)

Made in the USA
Middletown, DE
21 July 2022

69831910R00038